True Stories of Animal Heroes

Talala

True Stories
of Animal Heroes

Talala

Vita Murrow

Alexandra
Finkeldey

Frances Lincoln
Children's Books

In the west of India sits Gir National Park. Its wilderness is home to many animal families. Hares and porcupines swish in the grass. Tortoises and pythons slide in the soil. Eagles and vultures soar in the sky. And big cats—lions and leopards—lead them all.

The park was once home to an extraordinary leopard cub. Her name was Talala.

One night, when the moon climbed in the sky, and the animal families gathered for bedtime, tiny Talala wandered into the park. She was the sole survivor of her leopard clan, with no one to escort her.

As the other animals popped into nests, dove into burrows, and curled up in dens, Talala—who slept during the day—walked through the park. Eyes wide, she took it all in.

Talala listened to birds singing lullabies. She noticed furry animals having bedtime snacks. And she heard river animals splashing nearby.

The animal families
seemed wonderful to Talala.
Even though she was only a little
leopard cub, she set off to find a
group she could fit into.

Talala followed the sound of a lullaby to a tall tree. She liked to climb and moved her padded feet to the top. There, the owl family was gathered in a nest. She sat beneath them and listened to their song. It was lovely, but Talala didn't understand the language of the owls, and so she climbed back down.

Talala sensed in her whiskers that animals were grazing. She tracked the scent to the grasslands, where the antelope family were nose-deep in sweet

The elders helped the little ones reach hidden blossoms for a sweet bedtime treat. Talala tasted one, but it didn't taste good to her.

Talala walked to the riverbank to rinse out her mouth. There she discovered the alligator family swimming around. They had rested during the day and were ready to play.

Talala liked to swim and she joined them in the river. But the alligators didn't play the same way. They swam in circles, dug tunnels, and sat in the mud.

Talala didn't care for mud, so she sat on the riverbank and felt left out.

With most of the animals fast asleep, the park was pretty quiet. But Talala's wide eyes spied activity under a tree. She went to investigate and found it was the lion family.

Talala listened and understood their sounds. She moved closer and smelled the air. It smelled like meat she'd like to eat. Talala padded over to the lion family and saw cubs playing just as she liked to do!

The other lion cubs tumbled over to inspect her.
They wrinkled their noses at Talala's muddy state.
Talala felt like walking away.

But then the tall shape of the mother lioness appeared. She lowered her big, soft face to Talala and began to lick her clean. The mud was washed away, and the tiny leopard was revealed as a spotted fuzz ball, not so unlike her lion cubs.

Then the lioness laid down, so the cubs could have their milk. They shoved and wriggled to get their fill. Talala sat to the side. After their milk, the cubs were calm and sleepy.

The cubs piled into a tower to stay warm. Cold air swirled around. Talala inched near to see if she could join in, but the cubs turned her away. Talala shivered.

Luckily, the lioness knew just what to do.

She picked up Talala in her mouth and placed her at the center of the cubs. The warmth Talala brought to the family made all the difference. She was the special addition they needed to stay warm during their nap.

From then on, Talala called Gir National Park her home and the lion pride her family. Each night when the moon rose and the animals of the park began their bedtime ritual, Talala took her place.

She purred, played, and roared with her lion clan.

She had milk with her brother and sister cubs.

And when it was time to cuddle up, Talala could be found right in the middle of the pile, keeping them all toasty, as the spotted heart of the pride.

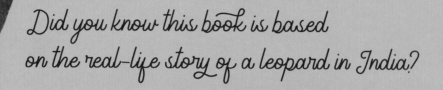

Did you know this book is based on the real-life story of a leopard in India?

There are many kinds of families. They can share things in common or be very different. Animals have families too. Some are called pods or clans, packs or herds, or in Talala's case, a pride.

This story is based on a real-life animal family that formed when a leopard cub joined a lion pride in Gir National Park in Gujarat, India. The park is one of the most essential, secure locations for animals in all of Asia, and is home to many amazing creatures.

Lions and leopards aren't known for living well together. They can be competitive and usually don't get along very well. Yet sometimes animals, just like people, break from the way things have always been to create something new.

Protected natural spaces like Gir are important because they allow animals to coexist in new ways. To learn more about helping parks like Gir keep running, get to know Wildlife Trust India and Global Conservation.

wti.org.in
globalconservation.org

Brimming with creative inspiration, how-to projects, and useful information to enrich your everyday life, Quarto Knows is a favourite destination for those pursuing their interests and passions. Visit our site and dig deeper with our books into your area of interest: Quarto Creates, Quarto Cooks, Quarto Homes, Quarto Lives, Quarto Drives, Quarto Explores, Quarto Gifts, or Quarto Kids.

Grateful thanks to Dr Dheeraj Mittal, Deputy Conservator of Forests Gir West Division, for their photos for this book.
ISBN 978-0-7112-6395-6
Published by Katie Cotton
Designed by Karissa Santos
Edited by Katy Flint
Production by Dawn Cameron
Manufactured in Guangdong, China TT052021
9 8 7 6 5 4 3 2 1

Photo Credits p29: Clockwise from left: Lioness and leopard cub credit Dheeraj Mittal; Deer standing in Gir National Park, India, Mukulendra Dutt / 500px via Getty; A baby leopard lived with lions for a month and a half credit Dheeraj Mittal; A lioness with her adopted leopard and biological son in Gir National Park in Gujarat, India credit Dheeraj Mittal.

Also in the **True Stories of Animal Heroes** series:

FLUFFLES
978-0-7112-6159-4

ONYX
978-0-7112-6145-7

STERLING
978-0-7112-6399-4

TALALA
978-0-7112-6395-6